LET IT BE BROKE

Also by Ed Pavlić

Crossroads Modernism
Paraph of Bone & Other Kinds of Blue
Labors Lost Left Unfinished
Winners Have Yet to Be Announced: A Song for Donny Hathaway
But Here Are Small Clear Refractions
Visiting Hours at the Color Line
Who Can Afford to Improvise?
Let's Let That Are Not Yet: Inferno
Live at the Bitter End
Another Kind of Madness

LET IT BE BROKE

ED PAVLIĆ

for Luka,

"real so thats' exactly and precisely what "

Peace,

Four Way Books
Tribeca

Library of Congress Cataloging-in-Publication Data

Names: Pavlić, Edward M. (Edward Michael), author.
Title: Let it be broke / Ed Pavlić.
Description: New York : Four Way Books, 2020.
Identifiers: LCCN 2019031756 | ISBN 9781945588457 (trade paperback)
Subjects: LCSH: Racially mixed people--Poetry. | African Americans--Poetry.
| Ethnic groups--Poetry. | Minorities--Poetry. | Identity
(Psychology)--Poetry.
Classification: LCC PS3616.A9575 A6 2020 | DDC 811/.6--dc23
LC record available at https://lccn.loc.gov/2019031756

This book is manufactured in the United States of America and printed on
acid-free paper.

Four Way Books is a not-for-profit literary press. We are grateful for the assistance
we receive from individual donors, public arts agencies, and private foundations.

This publication is made possible with public funds from the
National Endowment for the Arts

and from the New York State Council on the Arts, a state agency,

NEW YORK
STATE OF
OPPORTUNITY.

**Council on
the Arts**

PROUD MEMBER

[clmp]

We are a proud member of the Community of Literary Magazines and Presses.

For my family, extended.

Contents

2016 Summer Equinox (Police State) Revision: John Donne   3

i.   *A What Film*

All Along It Was a Fever   7

ii.   *Documentary Shorts*

Aesthetics: Quixotic Truth Serum   61

Boomerang and Yo-Yo and our Denial—Which Might Be More a
        Refusal—of the Inevitable Criminality of Consciousness   62

Achronological, a Chronology   65

"Someone's Getting the Best, the Best, the Best of You . . ."   68

June 19, 2015, I Remember Driving Through South Carolina, *Twice*,
        to Pick Up My Daughter on June 18, 2015   72

Subtitles: Love as Social Refraction. "I See You." Or, Evidence that
        Rihanna Has Been Reading Her Baldwin   77

"With Grief   With Fury   With Action"   78

Don't Ask: A Questionnaire   81

Instructions for Building an Alternative Fact Assumptions of Which,
  as We Know, All Arise from the Basic Modern Philosophical
  Principle: "White is Right" 87
Written April 27, 2015, in the Blank Pages at the Back
  of Bolaño's *A Little Lumpen Novelita* 89
The Rational Limits of Adoration According to
  Prince Rogers Nelson 94

iii. *The Interspective Lens*

The Interspective Lens: A Conversation— 97

Will the judges try to tell me
which was the blood of whom?
                    —Adrienne Rich, "The Phenomenology of Anger"

Imma be cool, Imma keep calm—
                    —SZA, "Sobriety"

2016 Summer Equinox (Police State) Revision: John Donne

And the American word
brother   resound ::
(father   son   uncle   nephew)

out (the)

law

Any black man's death diminishes me

I.   *A What Film*

"I have a need to make specific references."
                    —Kathleen Collins, *Losing Ground*, 1982

All Along It Was a Fever

i

A what poem. So I'm what?
Eight? It's 1974. I'm going to bed, scared,
in my bright orange, Jimmy Walker
J.J. Dy-no-mite T-shirt. Listening to the radio,
scared of what, I don't know—
my knee a dim-toned teepee under the white
sheet, Michael moving mountains,
Marvin dance with me, said, pretty baby,
or, later, Chaka Khan
you act so undercover; so under the covers
my summer body spilled thin
as the distance backward into a voice,
which is a distance spilled forward
and, no matter the mop, seeped through
the cracks in the historical planks.
Timpani. Ms. Khan sings "Clouds,"
". . . in the distance, coming to change my plans."

2015. "Are you Black?" I wouldn't *say* that. Sometimes the world says that.

ii

2010. I'm what gets off a dhow
with Fazul Muhammad's utterly peaceful
brother-in-law, and Binyavanga, at the lip
of a sandy, deserted island,
a stand of pines on a parenthetical dune
swept up out of a cirrus sea
above, off the coast near
the Somali border there being really no Somali border
between the sea and the sky.

Though you might think so.

iii

2013. Thanks to Hilton who wrote: "The something you want
to hear is the thing you already are
or move toward." When I read this I remember
hearing Miles Davis talk
about his listening transfixed
by the bandstand on the radio, said he
listened like the last of the living
fifteen minutes he had, each morning before
school in Alton, IL. "The black bands," Miles
said, "the white bands wouldn't come
into my body" and before he said that his eyes fell
into his voice a scratch rasp full of shadows.

2016. Can anything you already are be refused entry into your body?

iv

1983. In high school, I'm what that racist country boy
in Wisconsin called a nigger.
I'd only been referred to like that by racists
to my face a few times,
mostly from passing cars and almost always while in a group,
and we'd go crazy and chase after yelling
until we weren't angry anymore, or thought it had passed.
We must have thought it would pass. But it didn't
pass and we were always angry. And, one day,
maybe it was 1978, James Walker Jr.,
we called him Bo, caught a drunk man we'd been chasing,
we were fourteen, fifteen, and Bo beat him and beat him
and, I can remember, one by one, the few of us who'd
chased the man, beginning to wonder,
(I remember the man's ruined face) and I wondered
if anyone else was wondering
exactly how angry we were supposed to be.
So that noun had always been plural for me, niggers,
and I still think it always is, really. Really, what?
Plural. And of course I'd been called that in the other way many times
too by friends who thought it meant a love that hurt
in a way the rest of the world couldn't

name and so couldn't hurt, who knew it meant singular in a way
that's always plural no matter what you do or what
you think, plural, no matter what the real you you think
is you thinks, that was before we'd been
taught otherwise again and again and again until again
began to mean madness. And, madness came
to mean a kind of empty plain—a region we saw people
enter—beyond anger. A horizon you didn't arrive
at but slipped beyond and gone and we'd
seen that happen. Some of us had felt that (plural)
happen. So, when that one racist boy
called me that, alone, just me, you know, but also that plural what,
I was surprised and I remember saying, "Well,
you're an asshole," also plural, and in some
brightly lit American, possibly Midwestern, way,
in the brightness of a falling that never stops,
he smiled, looked me in my face and said, "Yeah, but at least I'm white."

v

I think the early 70s for me must have meant what
listening meant, listening very very closely
with my body for sounds that echoed things
I felt but couldn't find in the world
around me, in my house. Do I have to say listening
meant music? When I was little I don't remember thinking
that the people around me in my house were white
but it turned out they were. Or at least that's what they say now.
And, it turned out they all left. That's what I say
now. And part of what scared me then was exactly that,
that they could leave, somehow, and still be right there in
front of me. They'd say they were there but they weren't,
which, for me, then, made me feel like I might be
crazy and which, for me, now, sounds a lot like people
saying they're white when they're not, all of which, then and now,
feels like being with people who refuse to come closer
than a few feet from where they're actually standing.
Or when I did find those things I heard
in music in my house, in me, in someone, I felt somehow
I wasn't supposed to have found them
and then, really, felt expected, somehow, to act
as if I hadn't found them which, I found out later, is another

kind of falling that never stops and just one other

way that *again and again and again* comes to mean madness.

My sister Kate made everything up but she utterly refused to pretend

that the things she found in her body in that house—could it be

the same house?—didn't exist. So, when she was thirteen, she left.

I mean left for real, forever. And, that thing that forever, that

kind of horizon-falling-beyond-leaving-forever

was so far away from me I don't think

it scared me then but it does now, then

being somehow much closer to now now than now

was to itself back then.

All this listening for the entrances and exits

from my body was work

I absolutely didn't know I was doing

but when I look back that's very clearly what I was doing. Child labor.

vi

1980. I look up and it's summer and we're what
ducks down if we see his big brothers. My friend's name is Darryl
but we all call him Bubba and his mama calls him Durl.
We're on the bus and then here come
Bubba's big brother Carrie,
no shirt. Down the aisle. Blue plastic Montréal
Expo helmet pitched backward and his fro combed
out so it continues the shape exactly where the helmet leaves
off and his hands slide along the cold chrome
rails above his head, sweat rivers down into the string-waist
of his loose gray shorts. Carrie Simmons singing:
"Am al-right, don't nobody worry 'bout me." We hold
our breaths but Carrie goes past without a glance
at us. And, now, no one will ever tell me that that's not a black song.

vii

Please believe me when I stress
to you that this poem is not a performance.
Please understand I mean
none of this to stagger or astonish you.

The table I'm writing and re-writing
and reading and re-reading
this poem on is made of planks of pine I took from
our bathroom ceiling when workers tore it out.

Those workers weren't performers either.

viii

2014. On the platform behind a bodacious and curvaceous
woman with golden, metallic slippers laced up
toward her knees and a skintight dress with the phrase,
BITE ME, circled and printed all over it. I step onto the 5
train at E. 180th Street in the Bronx. It's August 2nd.
I'm on my way
to Baldwin's 90th birthday celebration.

Someone with the voice of an egg stealer whispers,
"Yes he is, see, I told you he is."

ix

2017. Milan is nineteen. He texts me a photo
from 1988. It's a museum exhibit where he (now)
goes and where I (then) went to college.
The photo frames the front line of a protest
march: DAY OF OUTRAGE AGAINST
RACISM. Return Text: "Yes, I was in that march,
I knew Solomon, Yasmin
and Charles, others in the photo."
The fog of that time of fraternity
slave auctions returns. Brown faces, now middle-aged,
somewhere, appear and fade. Linda Hunter
appears, a white woman and professor
assaulted on stage by white racist frat men
during my African Studies 201 lecture.
Reuben Cotton comes to mind, who stood up
in class and called those men what
they were "white motherfuckers" and they fled.
Reuben who cut in with a group of us
in the mile-long financial aid line at the beginning
of whatever winter term, saying, "Hell, there's got
to be *some* benefit to being black up in this mug."
Reuben and a $75 check I received as part

of a class action settlement from the suit he'd brought

against the racists' fraternity in Illinois. Reuben,

a campus barber, as was I, who introduced

himself, sitting behind me in lecture, "Hey brother,

who cuts you? I always notice your fresh line."

And, again, Reuben, with his parents at graduation,

after years knowing him, the first *I* knew that his mother was white.

x

2010. A little less than a year before Fazul Muhammad
will be shot dead after refusing to stop at a check
point outside Mogadishu, I'm what
walks with his brother-in-law as, every fifteen
feet, he meets another old woman
on the streets in Lamu Town.
They greet by swipe-touching fingertips, open
palms over their hearts and then kiss,
tips to lips, and then, *poof*, away from their mouths
with their just-swipe-touched fingertips
just like the first-taste
gesture for the chef if you tasted something incredible.

xi

2015. Wondering if anyone's armed and holding
Baldwin's *No Name in the Street*, I'm what
walks into a classroom at the University of Georgia.
On my mind, the sentence
"One tries to treat them as the miracles
they are, while trying
to protect oneself against the disasters they've become."

Are you white? No, I've never said that. Sometimes the world says that.

xii

1988 (photo). And, of course, by that DAY
OF OUTRAGE, the worst thing that will ever
happen to me had already happened,
the year before. So by then the sky-all-up-in-ribbon-slack
black body of my dead best friend,
roommate, ace, had been cascading the veins
in my biography. Sleep and wake, that
blackness swam a thousand routes, upstream
through me, a wrong-way traffic
in everything I said and did. And I felt language
become impossible and it made everything
I had to mean invisible. And so now what
do you call that? Who can see that? See what? That what.
And what, do you imagine they would be, and what
would that make me, who might be there, each
morning, to see the impossible dawn in the invisible
mirror and wake me up. And who'd be mad
enough to tell me it was language—that impossible thing—
telling me to come to the mirror, open my eyes, and try on its clothes.

xiii

2014. I'm on a bus in no man's land,
crossing the Jordan River leaving the West Bank.

Though you might think so.

Amid wavering, homemade rockets of asphalt heat, I'm what
hovers in the shade of date palms
waiting for a taxi to Amman. Standing in molten blacktop,
I extend my arms pulsed by wings
of heat that blow upward and outward
and billow back over the border.

(1987. Rakim: "Constant elevation causing expansion")

2015. I sit with Mzée, my six-year-old son, at breakfast.
Netflix. Curious George. Later, at home,
through the ceiling, I hear him upstairs, HIGH low HIGH,
intone: "I AIN'T got no TYPE." I make the WTF
face at his brother, seventeen; Milan
hears him too. He smiles at me and nods
up toward the ceiling: "Rae Sremmurd."

So, you know, there *he* go.

2017. Mzée is eight, his big sister is seventeen. They ride
in the back seat with Rihanna singing, "Wha wha wha . . ."
And I hear Mzée sing to his sister:
"When I'm with you all I get is *waf-fles.*"

xv

2008. I'm what walking what random
street in Kolkata surrounded by a waist-high cloud
of street kids? Fifteen sets of pitch eyes, fifteen
stick-thin bodies dart into the path
of any twitch in my glance.

It's very clear *they* think so. But they don't know. So.

xvi

2015. My daughter, fourteen, sings Rihanna's "Stay"
at a local café. She and Milan argue
about music. I'm what tells him that Suci doesn't listen
to what songs sound like, she hears what
they'll sound like when she sings them. Milan nods.
Sunčana sings, "All along it was a fever."

These days if I'm speaking to you chances
are—consciously or not—you're tracking a play of shadows
across my voice. If you asked me
about those shadows and if I thought we were what
friends feel like I'd say that those shadows
are prayers of thanks for the music my children love.

Music tracking quite precisely and fully what
comes and goes from our bodies. Family songs in every room of the house.
And if I ever say "Turn it down" please understand
that means never stop.

xvii

2012. The tires hit gravel as I become what enters
a driveway in a sun-flooded Istrian vineyard
with my eighty-three-year-old father,
the owner's arms outstretched to greet us.
2013. Thanks, again, for what
Hilton wrote: "the true nature of difference:
something stupidly defined
so as to be controlled." I think the Istrian
vineyard owner, Pilato, thinks so
but he most certainly doesn't know
because it's never even crossed his mind to think so.

1988 (photo). Somewhere hanging back in the fog
of sideways looks and the false choices
of possibility's post-mortem in the university
Apartheid experience, there's a BSU meeting I went
to during those DAYS OF OUTRAGE, maybe it was
a planning meeting for the march? Room packed
with anger and the Reagan-era racialized soup of adolescent
desire, allegiance, and vendetta. Of friends, lovers
and enemies—sworn and perceived—I'd have during
college, easily seventy-five percent of them would have been
in that room. And, when (I forget his name) asked me
to leave, the room comes as clear as any impossible
necessity in memory does and so does the perception come
clear of those who liked me and those who didn't.
The fog burns off as it does when vision and adrenaline
collude and there we are, and in memory I watch that what
become what's what from above: the enemies
look right at me, former friends and a few future lovers stare at the ground.

xix

1988 (photo). I'll go ahead and say this right away.
From here in the present verging into 2018,
30 years later, I can see that those black college
students watched me leave that room because, essentially,
every one of them needed to imagine
I had somewhere else to go, someone else to be.
In a way we were all in college because
we thought someone else had somewhere else to go.
And that truth turned out to be more
complex than most had any feel for dealing with.
Maybe the fact that I'm writing and re-writing
and reading and re-reading this now on these
pine planks from our bathroom ceiling means they
were right. Or maybe it means they were wrong.
Either way, from here, I can trace that tangle of right-wrongs
and wrong-rights upstream in my veins and I can
understand the need to imagine
I had somewhere else to go, someone else to be.

2012. I'm what's driving past the Lucky Strike plant
in Reidsville, North Carolina, with my wife
to the Calvin Graves plantation for a family reunion
on the land where her family was owned.
Our family. Her mother's side. Only the black
Graves came. Seventy or eighty people I'd guess. No one
I've seen here is white though the colors
of the black Graves who came here
and those who came along with
go from the color of this print to damned
near the color of the page it's on and
pause for a moment at the color of your fingers as
you hold this book open. Stones with no names
mark head and foot, graves of the slave
Graves they found out in the woods.
The stones don't say what
he was or why, after the war, Joe Graves, born a slave,
stayed. Maybe, all along, it *was* a fever.

xxi

Part of what my experience contains is the tone of someone
saying that that's not *my* family. Though
that what doesn't come home with me. That tone can't
mean it's not my wife's family, my kids'
family. And, if that doesn't make it
my family I have to wonder—
or cease to wonder—about just what
the fuck that tone thinks
a family is? That tone is an American
tone but it has its own cousin tones
around the world. I have cousins
around the world but this is all about right here
where I still listen for what comes and goes
in bodies and, as I do, I track that thing:
sly-eyed and rationalized being undead and on the loose in all of us.
That modern thing—or tone?—that's made an empty hallway,
a withered tribal lie—or national flag—
out of the polyrhythmic iridescence of human blood.

—dark energy: float this page wherever you want—

In 1972, Baldwin wrote: "Time passes and it passes. It passes backward and it passes forward and it carries you along ... through an element you do not understand into an element you will not remember. Yet, *something* remembers—it can even be said that something avenges: the trap of our century, and the subject now before us."

For years I sat mesmerized by the poetry of that passage. I recalled it and reread it over and over *again and again and again.* I didn't know what it meant until I realized that there are events, in the life of a nation, in the life of a person, which cause time to split, simultaneously calling forth the future while recasting the past in the fluctuating and anarchic image of itself, in the prism of a life.

Early August 1987, I was working in Los Angeles when my mother called me to say that my best friend and roommate, Riccardo Williams, was dead of a sickle cell crisis in Chicago. At that news, I thought my world went dark and my body disappeared. She said "Rick died." I remember I said, as one world ended, "Yeah? Rick who?" Nothing replaced that ended world. I drove to the beach. I looked at the disappeared ocean. I thought I'd become an absence happening to the world. I was twenty.

Maybe in a being beyond thought I worried—terror—that people go away when they die. Maybe disappearing and turning white were the same thing to me at that time? Given what I've found in this poem, it's very possible I thought that in 1987. It's possible I was that terror beyond thought. Maybe Riccardo Williams's death had sent me away? Maybe that's why there was no ocean to be found at the beach?

But, I hadn't been sent away. What had happened to me was an event, a death, the death of the one person (though never in life is there just one person) I'd have said was absolutely necessary to my life, to each minute, to the existence of time. So that death cleaved open time. It broke every minute. All minutes. I thought it was the forward future vanishing when, most likely, what I was feeling was that event reeling backward changing the reality of everything that had ever happened to me. It felt like my body boiling inside my body. Everything changing since I was born, changing in the place I was born before I was born.

xxii

1978. At times the what is exactly what
blood tastes like
the blood—your own
or someone else's—that comes along with learning
a language. Walking and talking smack talking
shit along with Chuck, Bo, Junior,
Keith and then John-John Jones says something
about "Eddie Ed said he give head"
and then my turn and I had it
all planned out had been waiting for this
but then me on my back in the snow with the blood tone
in my mouth before I can get out the last beat of
"but instead of Ed John-John's mama said
'I'll go right ón ahe—'"

Someone with the voice of the United States Federal Government
says "Yes he is, see, I told you he is."

xxiii

2013. Hilton Als: "Appearances speak not
of themselves." 1980-anything. Saturday Night Live,
Ain't No Jive Dance Party, WBMX, Oak Park,
Chicago. Party Ron Hardy. Farley Funkin' Keith.
Mickey Mixin' Oliver. Julian Jumpin' Perez.
125 BPM = 85 MPH up the Dan Ryan.

Hair on fire. (somebody's uncle who says that and it sounds like "hay own
fie")

Going to where? Maybe driving toward O'Hara
as much as O'Hare.

xxiv

It might have been a handout or our assaulted-on-stage-by-white
-racists-in-class our white woman professor of African
Studies 201 might have written it on the board. Possibly she
read it out loud. I don't remember that. It was a piece of a novel,
a quote, and I don't remember the author or the title
of the book. But, sitting there beside the slack sky-up-in ribbon
of blackness, ribbon of my own death, my all what
was owned by that death, I can still quote what she gave us
or close to it from memory. Professor Hunter gave
this to us but I took it for my own, I have it still. Paraphrase:
"I never wanted to dance with the sky gods.
I only wished that they'd make up with their ambrosial breath
for all that I lost when the ghostly brown figure of the last
person I knew slipped away from me, silently, in the night." I remember what
that felt like: a hammer made of written words. Chalk on slate.
I remember holding onto those words
as if they were steel bars and I was dangling over some bright black deepness.

xxv

August 2, 2014. James Baldwin is ninety. On that day
New York City names a piece of 128th Street for him;
as I walk to the ceremony up the east side
of Fifth Avenue (Uptown) on that day,
past the Scientologists and the National Black Theater,
and, in the space of a few blocks, two
separate, elderly black women
stop me to ask if I'm Reverend T. Allan Jackson.

Later that day I notice the name on the board
outside St. Andrew's Episcopal Church on Fifth Avenue (Uptown).

xxvi

2007. An eye bent over my shoulder,
I walk and listen to a broken stick of a thin man
with yellow eyes whisper murder
to me: sundown in Uhuru Park, Nairobi.

I speak now, so, I'm not what *he* sees though. So.

Somewhere, I've always got Carrie Simmons
singing Kenny Loggins in my ear. Timpani. Chaka Khan. Clouds.

(1980. Chaka: "In the distance . . .")

xxvii

1989—*the number. Another summer.*
I'm twenty-two in the back seat of a police cruiser,
the officer, calling in my profile
to the precinct pauses
on her radio, point blank: "Are you black or white?"

—*sound of the funky drummer*—

xxviii

2014. Headed back down Fifth Avenue that afternoon,
August 2nd, another old woman stops and asks,
she says: "Éxcuse me, sweetheart, are you Reverend Jackson?"
That night, on the phone, I'm on pause while
my seventeen-year-old son urgently explains a coded message,
"What kind of bridge did they burn
revenge in your mind when it's mentioned,"
smuggled by Kendrick Lamar into the ghost of Mandela.

I guess, in a way, the question is the answer.

Kendrick's question or the police? If I look back I can see
it's basically the same question come into
my body, that the old women of Fifth Avenue (uptown)
are asking me. What's been mistook? The question
about that question lives in my sons' eyes. At some point
when I was a teenager, I'd had to decide—call it pride—that the
question *was* the answer. As far as I can ever know,
that's how I've lived it—That chill, though, in an eye that still asks me
why? Maybe that's a shadeshift, a "cold-sweat hot-headed
believer," sung in my son's sister's

voice? Joe Graves, born a slave, who stayed, and

his great, great, great granddaughter singing what Rihanna sounds like

to her.

xxix

I sit with what I can imagine about what
the world sees when it looks at me,
what watches me, mine, that's to say, us, what
the world misses when it doesn't, what
I see when I look out, or back. Like what
motherfucker what!? What
voice to spill the body, this body, into? This my what body?

xxx

2003. I'm thirty-seven. Pulled over on I-94 north of Chicago.
So this is what
again means again and so we're what
waits. Police. Then two more cars arrive. Then a fourth.
My car is exactly my age. I know it can't go
fast enough to be stopped
for speeding. My oldest child, then six, asleep in my car.
And, while they circle (what?) us,
looking in the windows, one trooper, finally:
"We had a call about a child
in distress. Has your child been in distress?"
And, me, "Well, he's been asleep." Scared.
One by one the police leave. Then, it's just (what?) us again. Alive.

xxxi

The violence (always?) inherent in seeing
people for what they are, in history, which means
seeing them for what they aren't which
means not seeing them. And which means seeing
them which means us. Like, what
were they all screaming at what,
exactly, are they (you think it matters who?) shooting at what
are they really aiming at and there just ain't no who
are we without that what we are (to each other).
And it's not only the police.
Stop thinking it's just police. Every single American
institution aims itself at what
it imagines (because it won't imagine what)
goes on between us. Every single plural
one of us. Which us? Whichever us, all of us. At bottom,
the police defend, and the military
extends, and the prison system—which, no matter what
the law says, imprisons people according to what
they have in common—defines this basic American
institutional force: the genocidal (always?) system of individuation
which is policed by violence aimed at what
is between us. And so what's between us becomes

an unmapped, trans-personal power: the lithic
and illicit dark energy of modernity. That image which is us
which is the only image we have in history which is still ours

simply because the simplicity of its complexity is unrecognized in
history.

[I digress: white people have become what
they are not because they're pale and they're not born white.
Moreover this has almost nothing at all to do with Europe.
White people have become what they are—which is to say what
they're not—while they've been here.
They're white because they've allowed or convinced
or bludgeoned and forced the world—which for these purposes
means themselves or at least that's what a white person
would have to think—have allowed or convinced or bludgeoned
and forced the world to believe or say that it believes
that there's nothing essential in the space between them.]

And this is true for no one, which is the whole point.

With this two difficult and crucial matters of intelligence appear:
first, the only way to remain a law-abiding citizen
of this country is to agree to commit and replay its crimes

against the people around you, against the space between
you, and, finally, against yourself. And, the reason, for instance,
that the "nothing-between-them" people who work all day
convincing themselves they're white aren't profiled by police
isn't because they're what
they think they are, white, because they're not.
They're most often left alone because they're still
in their cage. Scared. Of what? Well, of what's not
white which is what they are.
The bars of the cage are made mostly
of the nothing between them. Until, which has long since
happened and happens again every day, "Nothing between them"
becomes a terrible hope: that the bars will keep out what
people really are while what
happens is more like being locked in—alone—with precisely what
people can never be. The bars are really wisps of smoke.
But, in this please understand that cities
have been emptied (of what?) by wisps of smoke,
schools, banks, prisons (and what
connects them) built and concrete reinforced, rebar
forged, from wisps of smoke. Wealth made
of smoke. That hallway you walked—did it feel empty to you?—
to get to where you are right now,
the emptiness you've been convinced flows either

inside or outside of your veins, all made of this twirling
historical smoke. Believe it or not at bottom the
police are there to serve and protect that
illusory empty space between people, to enforce that illusion
which no black person can vouch for.
Black people's presence—in peril and in power—
here has confounded claims
of such empty space between-nesses
and so that presence
is targeted. Understand that the crimes of the country
in this regard are what
is called normal—and so are what
is known as legal—which makes the actual
palpable living thing between
you and the person
next to you a strange, likely fugitive
—not to say criminal—energy.
Invisible to history, mostly visible only in the
images, in bodies ruptured, bodies policed and
punished because of it.
Here's an important note. That energy between
is fugitive and criminalized
because it's far truer than it is real,
which is why *this* is (what?) a poem (?) and why

you're wondering what
I am which means you're wondering who
you are—or aren't—which is healthy
and how if not why we're all at least wondering what
it means.

xxxii

Which what? July 7, 1968. Baldwin: "because people are always in great danger when they know what they should do, and refuse to act upon that knowledge."

So what? 1971. Adrienne Rich: "There must be ways, and we will be finding out more about them, in which the energy of creation and the energy of relation can be united."

Then what? 1972. Baldwin: "an entity which, when the chips were down, could not be located—*i.e.*, there *are* no American people yet."

All of this necessary to think about in a country that's busy day and night —including yesterday and last night including tomorrow and tomorrow night—putting you in charge of its lies.

xxxiii

And, no matter what,
still the intimacy (always?) of listening like rolling
a single raspberry seed between tongue
and tooth. Obsessed with that mortal sky. In the skin
of they lion. That sky under what
Earth? The rhythm of that listening coming and going from my body.

      —after M. O.

xxxiv

And so a blackness exists at the core
of the piece of that American thing
that hates what's at the core of the American
thing; that thing that's no thing that's
part of the code between us, and that's part of what
goes on within us, a line that's always already
been crossed—that doesn't exist except
in the crossing—into what
can't ever be bought and has always—constituent
in the woven and tangled fibers of what
American means—has always has always has always
been for sale. The price of the heartbeat
in every single plural one of us. Because part
(and only part, but part) of what
is black here became what
it is exactly—and hideously—because it was for sale.
And became what it is so so beautifully—if often
invisibly. And exactly because it was hideously for sale
it had to be what, exactly what,
was transformed into something that couldn't be
bought even when it had already been
sold. Sales pitch in the mic check,

sold out in the egg sac. Sure, but not bought.
And that not-bought what—
fibrous rhythm and half-visible fabric made of us—is the fugitive what.
Its fugitive status is also its power. Why? Because,
according to the stakes of historical power,
that not-bought-even-if-it's-already-been-sold and fugitive what
is far truer than it is real and it's
very very very
real so that's exactly and precisely what
indicates the depth of an unfathomable truth.

A truth that can't be bought, a truth at the core
of an American panic, in part,
and only in part but in part,
because of an American knowledge—terror—that what
can't be bought can't be shot. So *now* what?

xxxv

Undated fathom. Dream cop.
Question: are you the one with the son
who says he's in love   one
who says sister something like the way you say scissors   one
who says keeps saying stays steady saying
he's in love   afloat   one
with a sister-singer who carries 100 sold but un-bought slaves
hidden down in the hold of her voice

—SZA: "I'mma be fine anyway / I'mma be cool / I'mma keep calm—"

xxxvi

2010. Joe Graves's great-granddaughter,
my mother-in-law, and I out after a dozen ears of silver queen,
central Carolina sweet corn; at the counter, the women
are acquaintances: "Hey there *stranger*, this your son?
Would you like yellow or white?"
And Joe Graves's great-granddaughter,
to me: "I don't know, *son*, which do you prefer?"

We were told phenotype, the brightness of the bag,
was the question, the thing at issue; turns
out it was a secret, a method a recipe
for mass murder. If the doctor is correct
then ok it's true that,
by the time it was handed down
to us, the old mattress is half-composed of corpses,
empty shells of invisible insects
who lived off flakes of dead skin left by us, mixed
with those who slept here before. We all saw
that bright boy broke the bag, we saw him hunted down,
his shadow up against the wall. We all saw what
happened. If this is true, according to the authority
we've granted doctors and their dictionaries,
then it's true that our story
must begin and end inside the taxidermist's craft.
Unless, that is, the doctor was also among the hunters, unless what
happened to that boy while we watched happened to us, still
happens, and will continue to happen,
because what happened to him didn't happen to us.

xxxviii

This is true. Above, when I first typed the officer's question
to me from 1989—*the number*—in the police car,
I actually typed, "Are you black *and* white?"
How many rereads on pine planks of all this
was it before I caught it, the mistake,
and I thought about leaving it having finally
seen it, having found it, hell, having finally *made* that mistake,
and, while wondering "Which mistake," I
decided to change it back because that's not what
she asked even though that's almost certainly what she meant.
Last year, my wife and I explaining to her mother
what a gluten-free diet is. And, Stacey says, "Well Mama pretty much
you cut out everything white." And she: "*Well*, Ed, how do you
feel about that?" And me: "I don't know, *Mom*, what do you think?"

xxxix

The hard edge of historical light, it waits up for us
all night. Here's one brutal but apparently
necessary historical bargain: I said that the energy
between you and the person next
to you is truer than it is real. This is not a randomly
existing fact. It's a collectively and intelligently and menacingly
cultivated feature of our lives. Fugitive fact.
This puts you both—puts
us all—in peril, yes, but protects that energy between us.
If it were the other way, if that living thing between
us had become more—even as—real as it is
true we'd be more protected than we are
but that thing, that sacred being
-between would be endangered. The intelligence
of collective action knows, somehow, that that
kind of security is far more dangerous—the kind of danger
people become to themselves, then to each other,
the kind they become to each other, then to themselves—
than the peril in which we stand now. That's a hard
historical edge to stand near, real talk, that's the broken back
of a mother—black—skipped across a wit-quick crack in the sidewalk.

xxxx

And I know the popular-ista is the commercial illusion
of the necessity: to appear easier for people
to figure out than their own lives are. Otherwise everything—
like ever-climbing isobars, like Rakim like "constant
elevation causing expansion,"—otherwise everything one
writes becomes an accusation. And everything one
hears becomes a confession. So we do, in the shadow
of the auction block, we simulate the downward-sloping increase,
the commercial pressure of confessions. What else, though,
as in the shadow of a garfish, that stealth of itself in
the swift stream of that indolent danger? And Kendrick
asks, "You think y'all on common ground
if you promised to be there first?" And, a low heat
in the veins links all that ugly-beauty
what-business to some version of who
sees, who listens, how seen, who
reaches out and how, and how who tucks a chin behind what
shoulder, who ducks around what
corner hoping their voice disappears like Kendrick
like "What brush do you bend when dusting
your shoulders from being offended" like
who keeps what inside what

box inside of a box inside of a box like what
kind of "social-death" kind of box
the world won't come inside of like new breath
into clean lungs in an empty box
we keep in a box tied up with string and carried,
like Carrie Simmons getting carried away with Kenny Loggins
and me and Darryl ducked down so Carrie carries his big
ass on by, like we gone be alright, hands up
on the chrome rail and away down the aisle to the back
in the song we sing and that's what
song we sing, the black song we sing no matter what
song we sing.

II.   *Documentary Shorts*

"... improvisation comes directly from the rapport that is
established between the environment and ourselves."
                    —Michelangelo Antonioni, March 16, 1961

Aesthetics: Quixotic Truth Serum

Some people got to have it.
Some people really need it.
Do things do things do things
bad things with it.

Boomerang and Yo-Yo and Our Denial—Which Might Be More a Refusal—of the Inevitable Criminality of Consciousness

If we pretend criminality is a paradigm of connections
unsanctioned by institutional power
and therefore unimaginable by law-abiding people
in their function as citizens, and so if I say that
I think we could think
about the trans-national in a way matched
as precisely as possible to how we feel
about being trans-sexual, or any contemporary
form of consciousness being
trans-racial, you could call it, or me,
overwrought but I wouldn't call it
that, I mean, overwrought in the sense
of that moment when nothing means anything
and anything turns its mask inside-out
to reveal something just beyond the limit
of vivid and particular, I mean,
something of soft-loam and sunset
that signals something else just below
the horizon of itself, I mean, like
the schoolteacher in Marrakesh saying
to Roland Barthes "'I'll do anything
you like,' eyes full of kindness and complicity,"
and Barthes explains that by this
the schoolteacher meant to say "'I will

fuck you, and nothing else,'" I mean,
so the particular means invisible
to vision when vision means what
one does with one's fingers
when they can't be seen by anyone
as if operating, anyone, I mean,
behind a heavy velvet cloak, a drape,
anyone being the edge of fringe
that sweeps the floor of everyone
exactly and precisely in that
unmarked and insensate moment,
at times also called overwrought,
when anything means one thing and nothing else
and "acting as if" means "don't fuck with me"
unless you'll admit complicity, I mean,
will accept responsibility for the way I let
the bad guy win every once in a while,
I mean for injuries, past and future,
even ones from the place I was born
before I was born, I mean
wounds I inflict upon myself and those I love.
And though I feel very uneasy,
not simply to say conscious—or for our present
purposes criminal—in saying this, no less

to you, I should say that I'm saying this while standing

in the long shadows of things I thought

were injuries until I realized shadows

themselves, very often, are the injuries and the things—

many of which aren't things at all but people

acting as if—the people themselves had made my life

what it is by saving my life from the illusion,

I mean, if illusion means soft-loam and sunset

signals below the horizon, I mean made life alive by saving

my life from the illusion that it was mine,

I mean, the illusion that it was made, lawfully, of shadows it cast by itself.

Achronological, a Chronology

We said Octavia Butler wrote

sci-fi, it was the correct

answer on the test but we knew

it was a lie. Many of us, we kindred,

by then, had held twin-toned

hands and crossed up ankles across

centuries. Had played a game

called "Worldlessness," in Southern cities

like Chicago where, under a bridge

for a freeway designed to separate

the continents, one stood and listened

to a river overhead wider than

the ocean. Just like that like crushed metal

in the sound of slant rain

and we were the sound of the impossible

crossing that happens like midnight

in your mind. This morning,

23 July 2015, a front page story in the

New York Times details the

carbon date of goatskin leaves

upon which may be the oldest

extant portion of the Quran. Several

experts attest to the plausible

range of dates: 568 to 684. Other

experts agree with caveat:

the range specifies the age

of the parchment not the ochre

print on the page. Also on

page one begins coverage of Sandra Bland's

arrest and subsequent death

in her cell in Texas. In my morning print

edition, the one which can't be

un-published after the fact, after the jump,

to page A14, about her arrest

near the Prairie View A&M campus,

the article reports the incident

"occurred only a few hundred years

from the university's main

entrance." I checked online but

now it says "a few hundred yards from"

the entrance. On the test we'll say

the error was corrected. At the same time,

when we kindred, that's to say the living,

turn the page, and certainly when

driving, say, from Chicago to Texas, or hell,

from Texas to Chicago, and most

absolutely when told we're out of our lane,

we'll be careful, as ever, to verify the century we're in.

"Someone's Getting the Best, the Best, the Best of You . . ."
— for Prince Rogers Nelson

Maybe it creased and held itself open
in the sky, a pearly seam tongue-traced across sunset
on a thigh? Your death has clung to me
unlike other deaths, chance web, a filmy
permanence I walked through a week, a month
a year ago. Death today speeds past
what it knows, media flung: fifty-five blown
in Lahore, how many, eighty-six,
burned in Dalori? One of three
found in the woods, friend of a friend,
down the block. Who can help us—
"Till way next Sunday?"—bring on the Crab
Nebula? Who'll tell me when
that last one was mine? Didn't know you.
Never dreamed of you.
I was a teenager in the early 80s.
My father was an absentee bricklayer.
My mother worked her way up
to telling me to take down
the poster of you I had in my room, nude
in the shower, with a question
in each eye and a gold cross on a long
chain. Your voice told me sex
was something very nearby, a slowly-er

rage that pulls us out into our bodies
and beyond ourselves. That was you
and Meli'sa Morgan did "Do Me, Baby" too.
Toe on the pedal say wah wah say
beyond "Controversy," beyond sticks
and stones and black boys
and white girls whose scent, by then,
I'd contrived not to wash off in
the shower. That sacred means how it tastes
to hold someone else's life in my hands,
in my mouth, that a saint is someone some
danger I don't know who
tells me things no one around me
will say. I confess, as an adult, I'd sensed a ceiling
in the sound of your guitar,
I wondered if you'd begun to defend yourself
against something with it and if
so, what? I never asked myself about that. I let it be.
Call it technique, maybe privacy,
a ridge of invisible hairs along the edge
of your tongue, the visible shape
of wind across the lake. I think I know now
elevators must be called decelerators,
instead. I think I now know why

a lover might just need another
like a hole in your head. Did you hear
there's a re-make of you
in the Sahel, did you know the Tuareg
have no word for "Purple," so the film's called
"Rain the Color of Blue With a
Little Red in It." Let's forget
the taste out your mouth you came in here with.
Don't cry, scream: It doesn't matter
if it matters! Lost in a tiny body that swallowed
a huge country trying to live
without a word for pain. You held a lot
of us together, man, together
in ways we'd been warned about by
careful people hell-bent on ensuring the silent shape
of our deaths, you pulled millions of us out
beyond our bodies and into one another. So now
what? I mean what's now? Some 'nother numb new
tunnel to learn? Some Charlie Brown staring
down at his phone? Maybe now now can only mean
fifty-four and *me* blown, mean eighty-four and *us* burn—
Something now tastes like tin in the water,
now something speeds past but doesn't go away.
And, a hero, well, they're always tragic,

and soul and rock and roll and—well, made so
by we who watched you pass—when we could have closed
like one listening eye—like a wing of blue
wind with a little red in it, over a dune, like Minnetonka like
a sweet, swung-low ache, like down-slow rage on a sound stage moving
across the lake.

[Author's note: the final word in the fourth-to-last line of this poem
rhymes with toast and isn't the opposite of open. Rather—and if we're
going to believe in things like "opposites"—let's let it stand for the
opposite of what we are.]

June 19, 2015, I Remember Driving Through South Carolina, *Twice*, to Pick Up My Daughter on June 18, 2015

i

By evening I-85 south was a glossy tongue
and the churning clouds over
Greenville swallowed the sunset,
a collision of archetypal pain
and the lightning of the unknowable
facts, the near future. Suci's fourteen and terrified
of weather, I think, because she thinks
it means what happens outside happens
inside, too. Or, vice versa. Weather
in a house can low-pressure and go lower
and people don't really know how
low until it's your own lightning
and facts and no one in the house can breathe;
people squall each other, unknowable,
and tornado the plaster walls away;
she's watched some of that weather
happen and so it's probably
my fault that she's as scared as she is of the sky.

ii

6 AM I drive alone through a sunrise-storm,
headed north near Anderson, a fog of tiny
twisters steams from the pavement and I aim
the car through NPR news of another racist
murder, this time worse, a massacre, really,
and the search for the shooter. My stupid shock.
I can't *believe* I believe I can't believe this.
I can't believe I left a little brown girl, my daughter,
not two days ago, on the other side of South
Carolina, without a thought—a common-enough
thought in our family—of the day which is
every day when the room which is every room
becomes the room on the NPR morning
news and the stupidity of my shock lists itself
in all the eyes staring at all the shoes
and all the hands hanging at all the sides, the listless
-ness of people arriving too late, again.
The steam comes off this Southern road
like a fever and I finger my iPhone until McCoy
Tyner fingers the trilling behind Trane
and Garrison's thumb threatens to blow out

the bass cones and, as much as it steams
like "Alabama," I aim the car at the sound, "After the Rain."

iii

Sunčana clutches her pillow and distracts us
both tracing Justin Timberlake's career
backward across the low ceiling of clouds.
The deluge begins, again, the sky opens
as it promised it would. The semis flash hazards
and everything everywhere crawls slower
and closer. 'N Sync scrolls across the Bluetooth
readout, Suci sings along and I think about
my friend Jeff's neighbor, Terry, a Harlem barber
gentrified off Lenox Avenue and now living
with his wife and kids in the Bronx. One night
last summer Terry told me how he loves
to visit his family in South Carolina. Yeah? Yeah,
it's not like up here, man, down there, say
we go out to eat, I sit in the restaurant with my gun
on my hip. I look around me, another man,
even a police, and I think, ok, you've got yours
and I've got mine. Now I can't see what I'm aiming
this car at, I can't see four inches,
all the eighteen wheelers have dissolved,
red sponges blink and stream
up the windshield. I've got my daughter back

with me in this mad fact near the future,
where she should be, and now here we are at least
for a little while. I mean, yes, we're scared
but we're alright. Unarmed in this minute, this life.
And I see Terry nod his chin up, and smile,
his thick arm extended, palm up, onto
the table, showing his tattoo:
a precision clippers, an edger, cord coiled around his arm.
You know, he says, down there in South
Carolina, it's in the open, it's they got there's I got mine. And I feel free.

Subtitles: Love as Social Refraction. "I See You." Or, Evidence that Rihanna Has Been Reading Her Baldwin

"All of us know, whether or not we are able to admit it, that mirrors can only lie, that death by drowning is all that awaits one there. It is for this reason that love is so desperately sought and so cunningly avoided." James Baldwin, *The Fire Next Time*, 1963

"In our church, the Devil had many faces, all of them one's own. He was not always evil, rarely was he frightening—he was more often subtle, charming, cunning, and warm. . . In short, the Devil was that mirror which could never be smashed." James Baldwin, *The Devil Finds Work* (1976).

"After all, the first thing you learn in this country if you're black is a form of silence. . . nobody saw Malcolm coming nobody saw Medgar coming nobody saw Martin coming. These people who live in their mirror don't see what's coming." James Baldwin, April 24, 1986

"I needed you to please give my reflection a break from the face it's seeing now. Oh darling would you mind giving my reflection a break from the pain it's feeling now?" Rihanna, "Consideration" (featuring SZA), 2016

"With Grief   With Fury   With Action"

when we lose track of the person   not to be

confused with that democratic fetish

"the individual" when we lose track of that particle

that permeable pool of plasma

the person   and take human reality

to be a solid matter (most often

male) of people's (often enough clotted

into mobs   often enough mobs of so-

called "democratic action") . . . Jesus

Christ let's just call it conscious intention

lashed to the cleated post of mute

inheritance we need to be very careful

in that situation   when persons are

pushed (ultimately at gunpoint)

to feel that they have nothing to

lose and that can feel (though most often

it tingles numbly) like freedom

but it's not   freedom is never that

we must be ve-ry careful   more

careful than anyone can actually be

because it's dangerous when it feels

like anything's possible

but nothing can happen   very

dangerous when it feels

like anything can be put immediately

on display but somehow

nothing can be revealed   to live

in a world (so-called) where

everything's within reach but nothing

can be touched   *click*   maybe

it's a terrible truth (quite possibly

a truth of parenthood) that for any one

thing to be known (or touched)

everything else must be complexly

felt   as if thru an infinitely

sensate dilation   pure aperture   maybe

that is the open and awestruck light of love

and it's very simply never ever

simply just that   which is the spark of art

iculate speech   an S-curve pulls parabolas

thru a syncro-mesh gearbox   a sudden break

in low clouds off the coast

and into a remorselessly gray sea

of eyes pours a silver sheen   a glistening pool of pain

Don't Ask: A Questionnaire

What [let's don't
     say
     who] do
you trust?

And is it
     [let's leave
     alone   if you please
     the question
     of who
          altogether] is it
anywhere
near
you right now?

Not what idea do you trust I mean a thing [let's even
        disallow your fallback   gossamerity
        that ghostly cobwebness
        you've tolerated   too
        long   in your mind]

let's say that
a thing   in order to count
as thing   must fall
if you let it go—

or sink if cast away   even if
it may surface   sometime again
like a bone-flake snowfall
like that gossamerity that noose like a weightless twisted body
like truth in dreams

listing now the dangers
of looking
the other way [let's say looking
                but not seeing]
while [and here
        we'd pause and detail exactly how]

tolerance becomes romance

meaning while that thing that you call a thing
in your mind   as if

        [and here we'd walk—trace
        anyway, possibly
        take the M60 to the airport?—the route
        from here to there]

as if your mind were tethered   [even by stretched-thin
                                gossamerity]
                to your life
                your life to an actuality   one you trust
                [delusion alert: it's not]

meaning while you let go that thing
you call a thing
and that thing it just hovers there   unthingingly   in mind

in that space you now know
is mind
that thing you know now
is no thing

so no not that not-thing no   I mean a thing you know
by texture   trust by touch

no not fingers
[ok, now let's only allow things to be things if you trust

them
by tongue by press by salt and

solution]   and so you may know who you are

by the taste-shape
of the letter   even if approximate
by the shape you assume   [when I ask
                you what I'm not
                ever supposed to ask you]

[I mean   ask you   about things
        like trust]

when you're alone
like you
imagine you are
right
now when your tongue pulls you down   again   to go there

Instructions for Building an Alternative Fact Assumptions of
Which, as We Know, All Arise from the Basic Modern Philo-
sophical Principle: "White is Right"

.

Evidence

Interviewed during the second week of the Australian
Open, 2017: Serena Williams: "I always want to win,
but if I have to lose
to anyone I want it to be Venus."

Alt-Fact

Chris Evert speaking before the final match
of the 2017 Australian Open in which
Serena Williams played Venus Williams:
"I played my sister three times and if there
was one person I hated most to lose
to it was her. And, I know Serena feels the same way."

Evidence:

Venus accepting the runner-up trophy in
the 2017 Australian Open, having lost the match
to her little sister: "Serena Williams, that's my little sister
guys . . . Congratulations Serena, your win has always
been my win I think you know that. . . ."

Evidence:

Serena Williams accepting her twenty-third Grand Slam champion's
trophy after the match: "I really would like to take this moment
to congratulate Venus, she's an amazing person, there's no
way I would be at twenty-three without her there's no way I would be at
one without her, there's no way I'd be anything without her
she's my inspiration she's the only reason I'm standing here
today and the only reason that the Williams sisters exist."

Alt-fact

Post-Match News, Sports Center, ESPN Anchor:
"As everyone knows, it's the hardest thing in the world to lose to a
sibling."

Written April 27, 2015, in the Blank Pages at the Back of Bolaño's *A Little Lumpen Novelita*

And with Baltimore going up, on
a Monday, if I asked will it fly high like a bird
up in the sky and you heard
Billy Preston's voice as much as
any sparrow in your eye it'd be
because simile is simply cinema,
the screen upon which we watch
the language we use projected,
a screen we stand behind
and from around the back
of which we can never find our way
in front, I mean without
each other, I mean, as individuals,
like owners of property, like
amputators of senses, like
those who think they're protected
by the forces that assault others,
I mean, each other, by which I mean
not *each* other but all of us,
a screen we stand before and from
around the front of which we
can never find our way back,
I mean back together, I mean, like
we never were, I mean, like

when strangers insist upon referring
to us as each, I mean as individuals, like
others which we most media-ly are
and which we most immediately are not:
a mystery which, like, will it go
round in circles, from around the front
of which we go and from around
the back of which we come to find that we
had already arrived where we'd begun,
I mean, left where we've never been,
that screen of the uncanny upon which, upon
arriving, we just miss the last glimpse
of ourselves leaving, until
Monday night when it became undeniably
clear, at least in part, at least to some, I mean, like
a song sung to friends that ain't got
no melody or like that dance you do ain't
got no steps and you the music
moving me around, I mean, it became clear,
at least in part, for instance: when Don
Lemon and his panel of panelists
on that channel of channelists, begin to refer
to individuals as helicopters
shoot footage of a neighborhood in chaos,

that *one* neighborhood in chaos,
for live TV broadcast, well, I mean, like,
it becomes absolutely clear what
we're supposed to think chaos
is and what we're supposed to not think
chaos is and even more clear than that
that the channel of panelists are the invisible
and indivisible individuals
and that the persons in the footage
are being amputated from our senses,
from the history of our capacity
for touch, for feeling and that we're being
and that we're being and that we're being
assaulted by the force of another history,
that of a genocidal force that could be
thought of, I think productively,
as a force of individuation, which
I think could be thought of,
productively, as chaos, a productive
and destructive chaos whereby
we're forced to buy, or rent if we
can't afford to buy, or borrow
if we can't afford to pay, I mean,
right now, to watch the uncanny movie

of our lives and convince
ourselves that our arrivals are departures,
that our departures are arrivals, I mean,
both of which in any case
we just missed and that that's the reality
and we the infringement upon that reality
which, I mean, if that's how we watch
our own—let that stand—
lives then that says something very sinister
about how we relate to anyone else, I mean,
which packages the world upon, behind,
in front of a screen of language beyond feeling
and puts the world in a pyramid
of boxes marked individual
which by now we can see is a screen
as much as a word and, when
brought to a boil, when push comes
to shove and practice surges across the line
into practical action—I mean, did anyone
else just see the young man, or woman, hood on
mask up standing outside the CVS at Penn
and North and shot by an individual
lens hovering a thousand feet above his or her head,
as he or she stood stock still before a small

pile of something on fire, straight up, smoke in
a complex of twisters and he or she standing
arms outstretched and waving them slowly and exactly as if
preparing to take flight underwater or as if
conducting a symphony, as if listening,
possibly to Marion Anderson
singing "Ave Maria" or possibly to Phillip Bailey
singing "I'll Write a Song for You" or,
who knows, to The Weeknd singing over Satie's
"Dances de Travers"—
I mean, did I see that because, for all the talk
of individuals on the panel of channelists
no one said one word about that underwater
maestro doing, as if enraptured, his or her own beautiful
thing, so, I mean, in likeness of light in lenses like
those and actions like these,
just as much or more than anything else,
and in light of chaos, as us, as a historical force, we can see,
and not from a thousand feet above our heads,
that the word practical has to mean just
about anything our practice puts into the world and the word
individual probably just means legally—let that stand—culpable.

The Rational Limits of Adoration According to Prince Rogers Nelson

Well, maybe not the ride—

III.   *The Interspective Lens*

"The impromptu means chance. It is also definitive. What I wanted was to be definitive by chance."
                    —Jean-Luc Godard, 1962.

The Interspective Lens: A Conversation

it was morality   archaic species of sub-thought
some thought :

if one can't put the private self into public view
or an intimate sound into anonymous

ears   all your work in the incipient stupidity of solitude
will rat you out snitch your name

to the talc police of isolation   bet it

a conversation happens
amid many many conversations : some said:

cruelty the result of stupidity   the result of generic
intelligence   meantime others said: intelligence

that results in
cruelty can be thought
of as stupidity :   and others still:

we thought he was motionless but he was turning   the same
speed as the space around us   he was dancing   maybe   an illusion
of freedom
from the violence of certainty

we arrived at dusk   just enough light to sweep up
the scatters from the vacant year   a blue translucence

of tiny wings strewn   the room   dry behind the shelves   in
piles of three
the empty husks of scorpions   still fierce but empty

of life   elsewhere of life   one in an ancient halo

of her weightless young   likewise empty   me: come here and look
you: I don't know and I don't want to know   but you can

go on   I'm here   and nothing is listening to us

the initial image of the morning   an osprey in prophetic
protective
gestures   you: you'd have thought its wing was broken

you: last night   our first in this empty house
in this near-empty village   you: you took me

all wrong you know   or maybe I did or have?

me: most likely somewhere in-between most likely meaning maybe
you: in-between what?

me: meaning maybe human enough   meaning here we are

you: meaning what now?

                  me: "meaning what now?" is exactly what
                  human enough   is exactly what
                  meaning: exactly what "here we are" means
                  as means to meaning

we bought ice poured it into the plastic shopping sack   used a leather
shoe lace from your work boot   tied it all shut tight around the glass

throat of that simple chardonnay

from Istria   we splashed it on our faces   rinsed our mouths
of dust
from the road to Buzet

a preparation for the longest conversation

the history   *short*   of our kind   the long long conversation
be patient   we're talking about contact :
where patients   be talking contact :

the fantastic the elastic brevity   of a human eye

me: things we'd have to talk about to talk about—   you: I don't talk
to you   I talk to things I could never know about

you:

sustenance exiled with fugitives from bins of wheat
railways privatized and pirated

silos positioned along the border   talk like the last night
we sailed to Somalia where there's no border   (you

noticed)   and no police   (I added) between
the sea and the sky   you talk and stop still as a bangle'd lace

of chain on a sprained ankle in freezing rain   me: here
means bought on borrowed time

you: means on the *verge*   your profile across an upturned spoon

a sounddome of talk in a faint breeze   a still fan

an underwater eye open to a waver of flame above the lip of sky

talk of those   all those   populated and on the rise
inside our bodies   policed by the steady drone

the opportunistic fervor of the age   their age
our age all ages maybe   that spill across the spine

like a bow gone cat gut down the skeletal shinbone
of the master cellist   its shadow an eye in a needle

visions of disasters planted whence
their sanctioned traffic through us like a vow

says he do but means she don't   that sings she
will but hum he won't   for lifeboats halo'd around

the gone-hull   down to memories
of weightlessness all memories cast the experience of weightlessness

the poet's at the movies   one eye on the man coming through
the entrance   the other

eye on the route to the emergency marked :   EXIT
the world absent

from our young all fruit-terror all ripe-pleasure
our young absent from the world

the border (absent) between flesh and rind

a stroll ashore sure but on-guard   cut-purse and pick-pocket
the old woman warned you : showed you the asp

she'd slipped   a silent shriek
in her carry on   you: she recognized us   stowaways

enthronged by touristas   a village of scorched stones behind her eyes

all night in this forgotten house   you: by who?
you: futurity fool   me: the ends

of Earth   diver   miner   searcher
of extremities (foresworn) at which fixities (enshrined) loosed

loose like failed elastic and made its way   ours
you: futurity is fugitivity, bet *that*—

me: for chaos   and you: for another round
down and around of being unbound

Rukeyser's note about faith in division : "a trance
of shattering"   the danger of that   the danger of not that

the lost border on the loose   the culture : the lethal
and the criminal career of blood

(plus sundry additives) in our veins
Medgar Malcolm Martin / Michael Whitney Prince

newfound body count of what's lost: our post-boom
our generations' greatest performers

all dead   addicted

(meaning beholden) to killers
of pain   the new crosshairs in the American

(meaning in the global) spotlight   all that prayer
was it merely for eclipse?

you: fuck eclipse   and would you please define "merely"
(1994) a friend   you knew her

she wrote: *Have you ever felt nothing?   That is what war is now*

—Okay, it's state TV : late night : newsreel in—as far as we could tell—
probably Bulgarian dubbed into Romanian—

no idea if it's historical or breaking   or broken as far as
we'd been told   as far as   we'd dare say

        the springboard tongues into open space
        crenellated espresso air and eyes
        (yours) alight from Balkan nicotine
        me: can I say I was wrong about
        you?   you: say what you need to say
        if I want I'll hear what I need
        you to mean   a physicist with fingertips
        dipped in scented wax could work this
        out from there one finger across her belly   easy as this here

you: open me   let the night in   let all this (whatever else)
happen
in the in-most   let it (meaning us) be body-known beyond

the brackets   you:
if this be feminism (Rich   Lorde)   make the most of it (Rihanna)

          interspection : it's a tradition, too, you know
          those intricate and soluble techniques
          of tenderness   tongue an eleventh
          finger   its singular sight :   taste

          its eel's twist its snail's pace   where would you be without
          them?   me: them?

          you: ok, without us

          me: but us meaning what?
          you: us meaning in thrall to the corner where gestures
          of gentleness meet up with the lost myth of repeatable behaviors

Tennessee Williams could have spent all night in this empty town square
—stage directions—an actor's motivation

What we're listening for is a way to end this conversation
before it plasters over   bricks up
to the hilt   the escape hatch—what we're reading for
is that one-word-too-many that pulls us past
the equivocal quiver (introspective)
and revokes our ticket to the Pooh-Bah's banquet in

New York City

you: I mean take Bolaño   I mean what did you imagine
he meant when he wrote : "with a shuddering ease, as if leading a life
of crime meant always quivering inside"?

me: I guess I just thought that we were to assume that that
was simply what he meant   I mean meant in the title   by *Lumpen*

we came here for the near-emptiness   to be near emptiness   we
came for the charcoal sound of the night   we fell in love
with the sound of dawn : the shh-shhh-shhh-huh   sound of swallows
the mad braid of flown fluid

down the alley   the quick bank (hyperbolic function) at the open
window

the point of it all including love : to look back at our world   : the
success-ridden pyramid the mogul and the moth   the rampant rumors
of flame   flood lights trained on the spotlight honed in on search
lights in an arc

all set up   somehow   in advance of the marrow-crash
maps found tattooed
on the soles of the intern's feet   x marks the spot   the slave
name the place to dig the marrow gap between : us

us: yes marrow gap   the target :   sniper shot
serrated bowie lunge ace-boon with the body bomb blinked
at the airport bar and thought I saw another plane crash
log on password a numb syringe laced with mind-strobe

[the blue light dimmed for take-off]

us: code word   you: isobars in the pressure inside your mouth
that pressure isn't yours

me: you mean that by the time everyone's saying it   whatever it
is   whoever they are   it can only mean what no one will say

like ok like if I said   say   lithic   and you'd think I meant hard
or maybe cold but in fact I was only trying
to say smooth   you: without saying smooth

you: that's exactly what I mean   say it

me: "lithic" in a world where   for instance   "sir" means "don't
shoot me"   and where "don't shoot me" means "history
motherfucker" and where "history motherfucker" means "I wish
you would" and where "I wish you would" means "I would if I could"

you: if I could that's exactly what I would   shh-shhh-shhh-huh

me: so what it comes down to is   to stand among them   our people
forces us to stand beyond them   you: our people, *them*?

me: so   ok so stand beyond *us*   as in in me beyond you   you:
leaning over me
my historical skin our bridge of the moment   you be on you beyond me

to a moment
when

        : I'll stand within me   *in-tremity*   and you come

find me   me: yes! you know   words can do that

you: words—   you: again?

me: a life sees a life   a one   a many   you: hand me that
slippery bottle
I'll hand you a story   :   one has to love words   *hand*   *story*

a liquiddark mind of windrhythm : swallows in the alley
one must love words
enough to love something (you: someone?) else   more

or else :   the circles collapse
like crooked banks, like perfect curves   like swallow-sound

—her story—

granular night of crepuscular dark   words like light become
dangerous when collected on skin

left exposed   when left to glow in the sun-blonded hairs
on a forearm   so we brushed free of words

words : some wine and dine dust   some mine and find us
his was an act ill-informed a tin-tinctured act
of our invisible se
                        lves when invisible means unfor
given   if and when recogn

      ition means self and self becomes a synonym for irrelevance

—her story (vol. 2)—

irrelevance is seldom hence: the synonymatic like sin and them in
the attic   like cinnamon

for an addict   we've all seen all that happen

all which becomes a wall if by wall all we mean is the practice of larceny
and so we marched
soul clap   we prayed for rain   for silent wings of flame

me: end of the day   we're modern

you: what you mean we?   you: you mean *the* we   you mean that *we*
the touch-blind the bet the ranch on the judgment of enemies we?

me: yeah   I mean we the synonymaniac   I mean all of us dust

—her story (vol. 3)—

"It wasn't so much the shape of the flesh   the body contour
nor even the rush from her nudity   but rather   <<he said>>
the beauty the death-deep beauty of her cobalt-inflected blackness"

A guard said this to his friend—one of them was on break—while the other waved
us along up First Avenue   waved absently with his arm   AR-15
citizen issue   slung over his shoulder

          me: waved along to where?

                         shh-shhh-shhh-huh

          you: to where we were separated   and loaded onto the trains

—his story—

Masqualéro : masks exchanged :

When I was little my father was never home   away on construction jobs
I remember the ash   I thought it was us

on the floor of his truck when he'd visit home   I remember
Land of Lincoln on the plates   I remember a thought

—Can you visit home?   I thought it was dust

At dinners while he was gone: my sister was eight she'd pray: "Our father
        who works in heaven. . . ." (This told to me : I was three)

—quiet voice in the living dark   our story—

why do I do this   like this   to you?   me: I mean for real
you: you mean in life?

me: because my dreams are blown beyond all symmetry
so I do this like this

for real   in life   in our life   so that never again will it be
in my dreams   done this way   by me to you

this like this   nor this done like this   by you to me
in our life

you: you mean for real? me: yes   I mean in life
so then when I come off

the dock and into the warm water that surrounds
the invisible water of our body heat—our sleep—so from below

I can scan the surface

                                        of what's lost for something else or else

—quiet voice in the living dark   our story (vol. 2)—

[image: you take off your life and it turns inside out like if you remove
        a too-tight rubber glove] : that—*thwack!*—sound followed
        by swallows

time signature of evaporation: an interior turned out

you: you mean scan the surface *for* what's lost   for something else?

me: no I mean to scan   from below   the surface *of*—
I mean *of as if*—   I mean *when if is a fist*—

you: that's what you mean by   or else?

me: yes that's exactly what I mean   by us   dust

Acknowledgments

The author would like to thank editors of the following publications for publishing poems contained in this book: *American Poetry Review*, *Boston Review*, *Heroes are Gang Leaders – The Gianthology*, *Michigan Quarterly Review*, the PEN Poetry Series, the Academy of American Poets, and PBS Newshour.

Also many many thanks to the whole family at Four Way Books, especially Martha Rhodes, Sally Ball, Ryan Murphy, and Clarissa Long, for the work—far-sighted and close-up—bringing this work into shape and into the world.

Ed Pavlić is author of eleven books of poetry, scholarship, fiction and nonfiction. His most recent works include *Another Kind of Madness: A Novel* (2019), *Live at the Bitter End* (2018), *Who Can Afford to Improvise?: James Baldwin and Black Music, the Lyric and the Listener* (2016), *Let's Let That Are Not Yet: Inferno* (2015) and *Visiting Hours at the Color Line* (2013). Author of pieces in over sixty magazines and journals, most recently *Boston Review, Callaloo, Harvard Review,* and the *New York Times,* Pavlić is twice winner of the National Poetry Series Open Competition (2012 and 2015) and the *American Poetry Review* / Honickman First Book Prize (2001). He is Distinguished Research Professor in the English Department and in the Institute for African American Studies at the University of Georgia. He lives with his family in Athens, GA.

Publication of this book was made possible by grants and donations. We are also grateful to those individuals who participated in our 2019 Build a Book Program. They are:

Anonymous (14), Sally Ball, Vincent Bell, Jan Bender-Zanoni, Laurel Blossom, Adam Bohannon, Lee Briccetti, Jane Martha Brox, Anthony Cappo, Carla & Steven Carlson, Andrea Cohen, Janet S. Crossen, Marjorie Deninger, Patrick Donnelly, Charles Douthat, Morgan Driscoll, Lynn Emanuel, Blas Falconer, Monica Ferrell, Joan Fishbein, Jennifer Franklin, Sarah Freligh, Helen Fremont & Donna Thagard, Ryan George, Panio Gianopoulos, Lauri Grossman, Julia Guez, Naomi Guttman & Jonathan Mead, Steven Haas, Bill & Cam Hardy, Lori Hauser, Bill Holgate, Deming Holleran, Piotr Holysz, Nathaniel Hutner, Elizabeth Jackson, Rebecca Kaiser Gibson, Dorothy Tapper Goldman, Voki Kalfayan, David Lee, Howard Levy, Owen Lewis, Jennifer Litt, Sara London & Dean Albarelli, David Long, Ralph & Mary Ann Lowen, Jacquelyn Malone, Fred Marchant, Donna Masini, Louise Mathias, Catherine McArthur, Nathan McClain, Richard McCormick, Kamilah Aisha Moon, James Moore, Beth Morris, John Murillo & Nicole Sealey, Kimberly Nunes, Rebecca Okrent, Jill Pearlman, Marcia & Chris Pelletiere, Maya Pindyck, Megan Pinto, Barbara Preminger, Kevin Prufer, Martha Rhodes, Paula Rhodes, Silvia Rosales, Linda Safyan, Peter & Jill Schireson, Jason Schneiderman, Roni & Richard Schotter, Jane Scovell, Andrew Seligsohn & Martina Anderson, Soraya Shalforoosh, Julie A. Sheehan, James Snyder & Krista Fragos, Alice St. Claire-Long, Megan Staffel, Marjorie & Lew Tesser, Boris Thomas, Pauline Uchmanowicz, Connie Voisine, Martha Webster & Robert Fuentes, Calvin Wei, Bill Wenthe, Allison Benis White, Michelle Whittaker, Rachel Wolff, and Anton Yakovlev.